NEW YORK CENTRAL'S MERCURY

THE TRAIN OF TOMORROW

by
Richard J. Cook, Sr.

Rt. 4, Box 154
Lynchburg, Virginia 24503

FRONT COVER:

This original painting by Andy Harmantas shows the *Mercury* in all its streamlined glory westbound out of Cleveland Union Terminal sometime in the 1930s. The early morning light and the slight smog of the city obscure the famous Terminal Tower, looming in the background.

Library of Congress Catalogue Number: 91-65122
ISBN Number: 0-9622003-4-4

Typography & Layout by Thomas W. Dixon, Jr. & Carolyn B. Dixon

Printing by
Walsworth Publishing Company
306 N. Kansas Ave.
Marceline, MO 64658

Table of Contents

This book is dedicated to my wife, Nola, who has had to put up with railroads and railroading in her life for over 24 years and still remains sympathetic and very helpful.

Richard J. Cook, Sr.

NEW YORK
CENTRAL
SYSTEM

THE TRAIN OF TOMORROW

CUSTOM-BUILT
STREAMLINED
AIR CONDITIONED

Serving Detroit—Toledo—Cleveland

It was a sensation in its time, a train that was a winged messenger of hope for a Depression consciousness. The *Mercury*, billed by the New York Central as a "Train of Tomorrow," appeared on the scene in 1936, a completely new streamlined train for the Cleveland-Detroit passenger business.

The new *Mercury*, named for the messenger of the gods of the ancient Romans, said to deliver his messages with miraculous speed, was a hit from the beginning. It was a bold move by New York Central and resulted in a great boost in traffic and immense public interest. People flocked to the NYC tracks just to watch the train go by, especially at night when the engine drivers and rods, illuminated by spotlights underneath, amazed all who watched the new train.

New York Central had approached well-known industrial designer Henry Dreyfuss in 1935 to design a new train. Dreyfuss, whose designs included fountain pens, doorknobs, typewriters, sewing machines, air conditioners and dozens of other everyday items as well as airliners and ocean liners, now was going to tackle a complete train. This was the first time that a big name designer was called upon to do so. Because of his innovative talent, unfettered by traditional railroad design background, he created a startlingly fresh product that became a classic.

In his book, *Designing For People*, (Grossman Publishers, New York, 1955), Henry Dreyfuss tells how he almost lost the commission from New York Central:

> The final designs were approved by the late Fred Williamson, President of the New York Central System, but when they were put out for bid the prices were so out of line that the project was cancelled. It was a heavy blow when I received the bad news, for the trains had been a major effort for our office. I decided to take the rest of the day off, and I boarded a train for the country. En route, traveling the railroad yards at Mott Haven, I saw theanswer. I got off the train, returned to New York, and suggested to President Williamson that some of the used cars in the yards might be converted. Out of them the successful M*ercurys* were built at one quarter of the original figure. The *Mercurys* have been called a turning point in railroad design. They were the first streamliners done as a unit, inside and out, integrating everything from locomotives to dinner china. [1]

In the middle of a brutal heat wave in that Depression summer of 1936, the *Mercury* was put on display at Cleveland's Union Terminal, Saturday and Sunday, July 11th and 12th, from 8:30 a.m. to 9:00 p.m., on Track 11. The train consisted of a streamlined class K-5 Pacific-type locomotive, converted especially for the train, and seven completely rebuilt New York City suburban coaches, including a round-end observation car. They numbered 1001 through 1007, were built by the Osgood Bradley Car Company in 1927 and had been used on the Putnam Division on the New York Central. These cars had an arch-type roof which readily contributed to the streamline effect when enclosures were added between the cars and at the rear of the locomotive tender. Tightlock couplers with improved draft gear were applied to allow smoother train handling. Each car sported a large winged Mercury silver medallion on either side to help add a distinctive note to the train.

"Train of Tomorrow" ad in the Cleveland *News*
(Western Reserve Historical Society)

A Cleveland newspaper, chronicling the event of the public showing, observed:

> With smoothness and grace, the *Mercury*, the New York Central's streamlined "train of tomorrow," glided into Union Terminal last night ready for the public's inspection today and tomorrow before going into regular service between Cleveland and Detroit at an hour's saving over present schedules.[2]

The train won additional approval that hot summer because it was air conditioned. It also helped boost the Great Lakes Exposition held on Cleveland's lakefront at the time by attracting many out of town visitors.

"I never had a smoother ride", exclaimed 18-year-old Suzanne Saunders, "Miss Great Lakes." "I'd forgotten it was so hot outside," she said when she left its air-cooled comfort.[3]

The next day, July 13, was a press run to Detroit and back. The Cleveland *News* reported:

> A minute or so after nine it oozed out of Cleveland bearing 46 newspapermen and a score of New York Central officials and experts on its maiden run to Detroit. The getaway of the *Mercury* is a new sensation in speed. Motion is difficult to locate, it just ebbs and flows like a ship in the tides. . . Jar and jolt, lunge and side-sway are all absent in the *Mercury*, and the collar doesn't wilt Conversations within the train, driving at 75 miles an hour, are carried on in ordinary low tones. Sounds from within have no competition from without.[4]

Newspapermen were impressed with the fact that, as Henry Dreyfuss observed, the train was as luxurious as a private club. No two cars were alike in interior arrangement.

The first three cars had ceilings of light gray tan relieved by a wide horizontal aluminum molding below the center lighting trough. Wainscotting was light chocolate. Seats were brown mohair with stripes running diagonally.[5]

Of the seven original cars, the first coach had a baggage room and a smoking room for 12 on the other side of the bulkhead. The rest of the car seated 40 in reclining coach seats decorated in a combination of brown with large "Mercury" headrest covers.

The second car, a full coach with a seating capacity of 48, featured a smoking room at one end, seating 12, and four seats, mid-car, facing each other. This tended to break up the traditional long aisle. There was also a built-in couch against the forward wall. A large photo mural of downtown Detroit covered the bulkhead above the couch.

The third car was a kitchen car with an 18-seat coach section in its forward end.

This left the next car with the freedom of being a full dining section. This resourcefully designed car seated 56 in the dining section and 6 in the waiting lounge. Diners in the mid-section sat with their backs to the outside (window) wall and faced the aisle. In addition, there were 12 tables arranged in the traditional manner. Because of the relatively short 3 1/2-hour Cleveland-Detroit trip, it was necessary to provide facilities for serving a large number of passengers quickly—breakfast on the westbound trip and dinner on the eastbound.

The three sections were separated by double partitions about a foot apart, having clear plate glass above the wainscotting. Cut flowers or plants were placed between the glass walls. The lounge area was fitted with built-in settees on either side, upholstered in light tan leather. The walls contained framed copies of Cezanne paintings.

The next three cars were operated by the Pullman Company. They consisted of a lounge car with a semi-circular bar, a parlor car with deep easy chairs situated around tables, and a parlor observation car.

The bar of the first parlor car, backed up by mirror panels extending from the top of the bar to the ceiling, was located mid-way in the car. Heavily upholstered loose chairs, built-in settees and sections were conveniently arranged on either side of the bar.

The ceiling of the car was flat and relatively low, which, with the vertical grain of the quartered walnut finish on the walls, combined to create a sense of unusual spaciousness. The bronze metallic look of the ceiling coordinated with a rust-colored carpet similar in pattern to

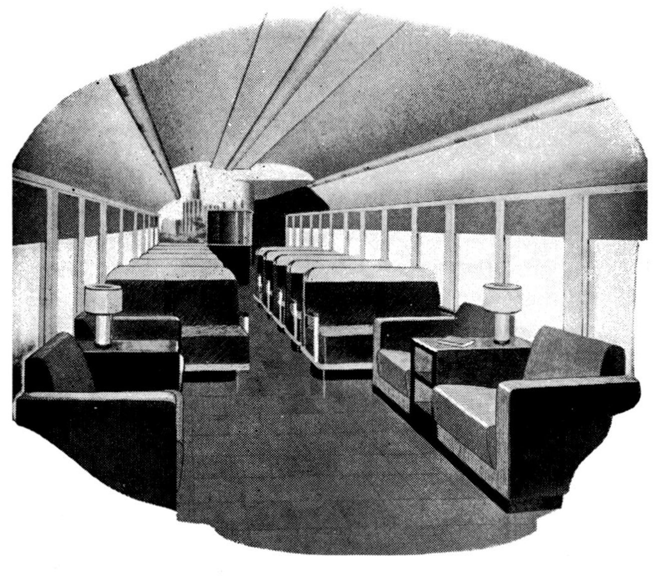

Coach

Lounge

Car interior views from *Mercury* brochure, 1936.

Diner

Observation

the one in the diner. Windows boasted light tan venetian blinds to create a quiet, subdued atmosphere.

Although the chairs of the full parlor car were similar in form, they were upholstered in a variety of colors and fabrics. Tables and lamps were conveniently placed for the 25 available seats. Perhaps the high point in the decoration of the car was a cloud mural with which the outside walls of the semi-circular compartment in the middle of the car were furnished.

The rear car, the parlor-observation, featured a fixed center settee built with seats for three persons on each of two sides facing toward the windows and with seats for two persons at the rear end directly facing the receding tracks as the train sped over the polished rails. There were two additional chairs in the observation section. The view was delightful because the windows were lowered by one foot from the customary observation window height. They were nearly four feet high. Rear-viewers were kept fascinated by the speedometer set in the center settee. The remainder of the car, with a seating capacity of 26, was similar to the preceding parlor car.

Vestibule illustration from 1936 brochure.

One other outstanding feature of the new train immediately greeted one when he climbed aboard. It was the large round vestibules, a single vestibule at one end of each car. The usual vestibule end posts had been moved outward to give a clear passage between cars of 5 ft. 3 in. The effect in the case of the two end cars, which were arranged vestibule to vestibule, was to create a rotunda of an unusual and welcoming size. When one entered the *Mercury*, he felt that he was beginning an exciting travel experience rather than a mundane train trip. The feeling was one of elegance and quiet dignity, much like that of a fine club of the era. The on-train crew did all they could to continue this feeling through superb, speedy and courteous service.

The exterior treatment of the train was a combination of medium gray paint with scratch-brushed aluminum trim, carrying back from the locomotive tender the entire length of the train.

The Pacific-type locomotive, on a design developed in 1926, was refitted in Central's West Albany Shops. It had a maximum tractive force of 37,600 pounds, with cylinders measuring 25 inches in diameter with 28-inch stroke. Boiler pressure was 200 pounds per square inch.

The entire locomotive was covered with a "bathtub" cowl, similar to the streamlining applied to Hudson-type No. 5344, the *Commodore Vanderbilt*, in 1934. The *Mercury* locomotives had a more rounded, tapered front and a more "stream-styled" appearance. Like the 5344, the *Mercury* locomotives also had their steam domes and sand domes covered, as well as pumps, pipes and whistle. All of this contributed to the smooth look of speed capability that appealed to the public eye.

The high 79-inch Boxpok drivers sported centers painted in aluminum with a black band separating the center aluminum discs from the aluminum rim and tire. Dreyfuss had installed three 50-watt and two 15-watt lamps under the cowling on either side to illuminate the drivers and rods. The effect at night was most striking.[6]

half miles east of Erie, Michigan. A resident of a nearby town, unused to a train of such high speed, was killed instantly when the 70-mile-an-hour *Mercury* overtook him. One of the passengers on this train, it was said, was Cleveland Safety Director Eliott Ness, later to achieve national fame.[8]

Dreyfuss's rationale for the development of his "Train of Tomorrow" was touched upon in his book:

> In our work on railroad cars for the New York Central, we set out to create the atmosphere and character of a fine club in the diners and lounge cars. This was done by installing the type of furniture, the colors and the materials expected in a club, but retaining, architecturally, the clean lines possible in a modern railroad car. We broke up the long passageways by placing divans and tables crosswise. We also used restful beiges or earthy

The *Mercury* at night, from *Railway Age*, July 11, 1936.

Proud of its bold and beautiful transportation accomplishment, the New York Central made sure that its new train was well publicized in newspapers and on radio. Also, the railroad, to commemorate the building of its modern train, struck 500 copies of a medal showing the date and nameplate of the train. These were distributed to each of the mechanics, draftsmen and designers who took part in the construction of the train.[7]

The July 15, 1936 inauguration of the *Mercury* proved to be so successful that a second section of air conditioned parlor cars had to be assembled to follow the sold-out streamliner. Not quite all went well, however. On the return trip the new locomotive struck a car one and one-

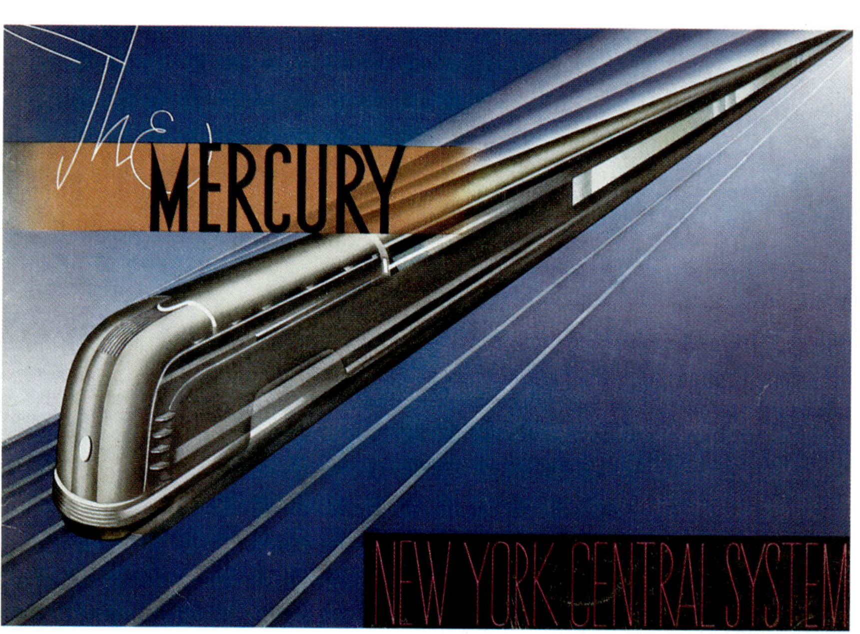

The New York Central System wanted to make sure it impressed certain important passengers, and to do so produced an 8 1/2x11-inch brochure in full color. (Western Reserve Historical Society)

> tones with bright colors as harmonious accents. Occasionally we used mirrors to give the feeling of width. As if by magic, the cars no longer had the appearance of a well-tilled cabbage patch.[9]

Another innovation in the *Mercury* was the installation of an electric eye between the galley and the dining car. The mystery of the automatic door seemed to frighten waiters at first, some of whom dropped their trays when they first encountered it. But they soon got used to this great helper.[10]

Travel on the Cleveland-Detroit route more than doubled the year following the *Mercury's* inauguration. *Railway Age* in 1937 reported that the *Mercury* averaged 290 persons per day and that 53,377 passengers were carried in the train's first six months. It became quite popular with businessmen, especially those in the automotive industry who shuttled between Detroit's auto plants and Cleveland's many automotive equipment manufacturers.[11]

The 164-mile schedule called for a Cleveland departure of 7:30 a.m., an arrival in Toledo at 9:15, and the Detroit arrival at 10:20 a.m. Eastbound, the train left Detroit at 5:35 p.m., arrived in Toledo at 6:35, and at Cleveland by 8:25. Sunday's eastbound schedule was set at 55 minutes later. In April of 1937 the schedule was changed to a 10:15 a.m. Detroit arrival and eastbound times of 5:30 leaving Detroit and a Cleveland arrival of 8:20 p.m.[12]

The train continued to be a hit, so much so, that in 1938-39 a second *Mercury* trainset was constructed at the shops in Beech Grove, Indiana, where the original train had been fabricated. It entered an expanded Cleveland-Detroit-Chicago service.

The *Mercury* locomotives, ex-Big Four (CCC& St.L) Pacifics 4915 and 4917, were supplemented by larger power, the NYC having learned from previous mistakes that more than seven cars required stronger power in order to maintain the high speed the schedule demanded. So Hudson-type locomotives were soon assigned to the Detroit-Chicago run. This new service began in November 1939.

The most distinguished day train in America is now in service between

CHICAGO and DETROIT

via Michigan Central Route

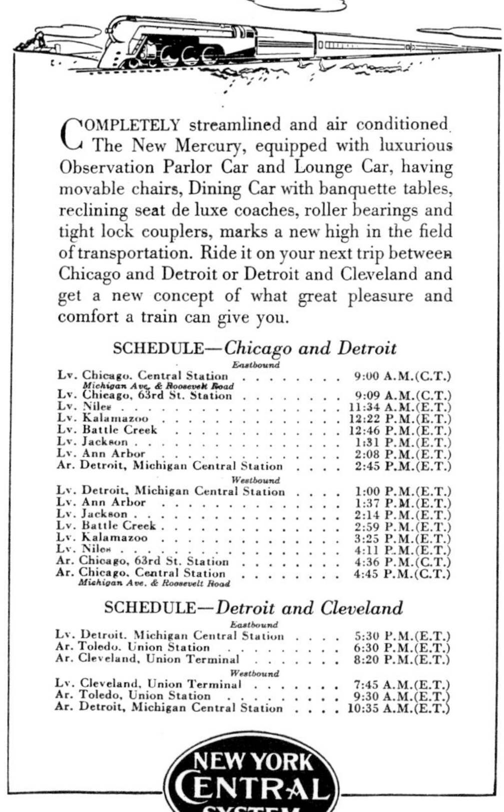

Chicago *Mercury* ad from New York Central public timetable of December 7, 1941.

The following comments, made by those who saw the train "in person," convey the thrill that came over people when they saw the Central's "Train of Tomorrow:"

C. Robert Bachman, retired New York Central train dispatcher and chief train dispatcher—

"It was really a fabulous train. The engine with its distinctive white rods was brought down from Linndale every morning but it had to be kept out from underneath the Terminal buildings so that it wouldn't smoke up all the offices and shops above.

"People used to go out to Berea (22 miles west) to watch the Mercury go by (at 8:05 p.m.) at high speed toward Cleveland, then they'd often stay to watch the rest of the New York Central's 'Great Steel Fleet' pass by—eastbound—as well. The Mercury led the parade of fast eastbound passenger trains out of Toledo for Cleveland and beyond.

"The *Mercury* was turned each night by pulling it, rear end first, west out of the Terminal to Clark Avenue, where the 'shuttle' (engine and caboose) would back it down over the old Big Four line to the old Union Depot where it was turned on the lakefront wye, then routed back to the Terminal via Clark Avenue.

"In later years the train was pulled farther west for turning: to Linndale where it entered the eastbound main and ran against the current of traffic under a train order from the operator at Linndale (CF) Tower. At Short Line Junction, the entrance to Rockport Yard, it was turned on the wye and pushed back down No. 2 track. The shuttle's Pacific-type engine then shoved the train into a coachyard track at Cleveland Union Terminal for nighttime servicing. An electric 'depot' motor spotted the Mercury on its outbound track early the next morning."

George Snyder, retired New York Central switchtender and brakeman --

"I was lucky enough to see that train at night at Linndale when I worked second trick there in the Forties. People would gather in droves to see that train as it went by with its engine drivers lit up. When the *Mercury* came in view at night all you saw was the black and silver drivers and silver rods flashing past you, then the lights of the cars streaming by and the illuminated sign '*Mercury*' on the tail end.

"When I rode the train I sat in the observation car and watched the speedometer get up to 93 miles an hour. The observation car was a thing of art. The windows were large and rounded and you could really see the view.

"I used to go down to the roundhouse almost every morning and every night just to look at the *Mercury*. Stall 23 or 27 she would be in. I remember they used to back it down to the Terminal every morning. I must have ridden that train at least 40 times.

"The longest I ever saw the *Mercury* was as a 12- or 15- car train. The Cleveland Indians and Detroit Tigers baseball teams used to travel on the *Mercury* for their Detroit-Cleveland games."

Bob Lorenz of Fremont, Ohio, commercial artist, specializing in railroad subjects—

I always thought it was a beautiful train. Some say that the engine looked like a bathtub turned upside down, but I thought it was the greatest thing on rails, and still do.

"One thing I do remember. Once in a while the streamlined engine would be on the Plug (Cleveland-Toledo local) through Fremont, on train No. 627. In fact I recall it came through for three or four nights in a row and so many people were at the station to see the engine that one fellow put up a popcorn stand. Then one night the train came in with just a regular Pacific-type on the head end. The throng of people all left in about two minutes and the popcorn man was not far behind. That was it."

Mrs. Zora Gumz, office manager for the Brotherhood of Locomotive Engineers Building Association in Cleveland, Ohio—where she has been for 15 years—remembers the *Mercury*. She is a native of Berea, Ohio.

"The train was a great attraction because not much ever went on out there. It was just a real big bang. All the neighbors and their kids would walk up to the tracks just to watch the train go by. It was a mile and-a-half to two miles to the tracks where we would wait for it. That was about 1937. The train was new and exciting and beautiful. You could see it coming all lit up. I get goose bumps just thinking about it because it was such a thrill for all of us. It was like the beginning of a new era.

"My father was just fascinated; he thought it was just the greatest thing. We would have friends come from Cleveland and one of the things they wanted to do was to go up with us so that they, too, could see the *Mercury* go by. We thought it went by very fast. At that time there were calendars and many other items that had the *Mercury* on it. It would often get mentioned in the newspapers, especially the Berea *News* which always seemed to have something in it about the *Mercury*. It was a big thing in Berea;

you would have thought it belonged to the town.

"I remember the beautiful silver and gray train going by the Berea station at dusk. It was just fascinating."

By 1940 the *Mercury* schedule was as follows:

Lv. Cleveland	7:45 a.m.
Ar. Toledo	9:30
Lv. Toledo	9:30
Ar. Detroit	10:35
Lv. Detroit	1:00 p.m.
Lv. Ann Arbor	1:37
Lv. Jackson	2:14
Lv. Battle Creek	2:59
Lv. Kalamazoo	3:25
Lv. Niles	4:11
Central Standard Time	
Ar. 63rd St., Chicago	4:36
Ar. Chicago	4:45 p.m.
Central Standard Time	
Lv. Chicago (Central Sta.)	9:00 a.m.
Lv. 63rd St., Chicago	9:09
Eastern Standard Time	
Ar. Niles	11:34
Ar. Kalamazoo	12:20 p.m.
Ar. Battle Creek	12:46
Ar. Jackson	1:30
Ar. Ann Arbor	2:08
Ar. Detroit	2:45
Lv. Detroit	5:30
Ar. Toledo	6:35
Lv. Toledo	6:35
Ar. Cleveland	8:25

Thus it was possible, if one wanted to, to make a trip between Chicago and Cleveland all by *Mercury*. It would have been a most comfortable way to travel, if one had all day.

On July 30, 1938, slippery rails and a stopped *Mercury* resulted in a crash that put the Detroit-Cleveland train's observation car out of service. At Rocky Ridge, Ohio, 22 miles east of Toledo, a fast moving *Commodore Vanderbilt*, NYC's second best Chicago-New York train, rammed into the end of the *Mercury*. Thirty-one persons were taken to hospitals. Although the *Commodore Vanderbilt* had slowed to between 10 and 15 miles an hour, it slid into the train ahead of it. The *Mercury* had stopped because it had grazed an automobile at a crossing.[13]

The observation car, the only car seriously damaged, was taken to Beech Grove Shops. It emerged as good as new several months later and replaced the old-style parlor observation car which had been substituting for it.

In the meantime, Henry Dreyfuss had won a contract from the New York Central for an all-new, completely streamlined *20th Century Limited*. This included a fleet of new streamlined Hudsons from American Locomotive Company in Schenectady, New York. As these streamlined engines began to appear on the system, they would show up occasionally pulling the *Mercury*. Increased business demanded more cars to be built for the trains too. Hudsons began to replace the famous "lighted-at-night" Pacifics out of Cleveland because the trains were getting too heavy for them. And the practice of running the steamers into and out of the Cleveland Union Terminal was dropped. Now it was a powerful electric motor which hauled the heavier train up the stiff grade to Linndale.

There is nothing like success to breed more success, or at least to tempt an effort in that direction. On April 28, 1941, still another *Mercury* emerged from the Beech Grove "wonder shops," this time for service between Cincinnati and Chicago. Although it bore a different name, the *James Whitcomb Riley*, this new streamliner was a copy of the successful *Mercury* trains, from observation car to the forward coaches and innovative diner.

Popular? No wonder it's popular! . . . Fastest service between Chicago and Cincinnati . . . Convenient morning departure from Cincinnati and latest afternoon departure from Chicago . . . Individual reclining seats, *reserved without any extra charge* . . . New from its streamlined engine to its gorgeous observation solarium car . . . *And all this for these low fares:*

	One Way	*Round Trip*
Chicago to Cincinnati . . .	**$5.90**	**$10.65**
Chicago to Indianapolis . .	**3.70**	**7.10**
Indianapolis to Cincinnati .	**2.20**	**4.20**

ROUND TRIP SCHEDULE

(Daily except Sunday)

(read down)			*(read up)*
8:15 A.M.	Lv. Cincinnati (E.T.) . . .	Ar.	10:55 P.M.
9:00 A.M.	Ar. Indianapolis (C.T.). . .	Lv.	8:10 P.M.
9:05 A.M.	Lv. Indianapolis (C.T.). . .	Ar.	8:05 P.M.
10:05 A.M.	Ar. LaFayette	Ar.	7:04 P.M.
11:20 A.M.	Ar. Kankakee	Lv.	5:45 P.M.
12:15 P.M.	Ar. Chicago (63rd St.) . . .	Lv.	4:50 P.M.
12:30 P.M.	Ar. Chicago (Central Station) (Michigan Ave. & Roosevelt Rd.)	Lv.	4:40 P.M.

James Whitcomb Riley **ad from New York Central public timetable of November 12, 1939.**

But unlike the *Mercury*, the *Riley* was an all-coach train, leaving Cincinnati at 8:15 a.m., arriving Chicago at 12:30 p.m., and returning for an overnight stay in the Queen City by 10:55 p.m.[14]

Not the *Mercury*, you say? In addition to those new *Mercury*-inspired cars, there were our two old friends, engines 4915 and 4917 back on their Big Four rails, sporting classification lights in accord with Big Four practice, and ready to haul the new seven-car train.

Before going into regular service, the *Riley*, like the original *Mercury* before it, was put on display at a number of online cities: Cincinnati, Indianapolis, Lafayette, Kankakee and Chicago. Back in 1936 the "Train of Tomorrow" had, in addition, made a pre-Cleveland tour of eastern NYC mainline cities and was put on display in New York City for a time.

Meanwhile, over on the Michigan Central portion of the NYC system, the passenger department, wanting to tap more Detroit business, persuaded the railroad to institute an earlier departure from Detroit: 8:30 a.m., and a like leaving time from Chicago. This proved to be popular. New cars in the form of Central's huge system-wide order of streamlined coaches were added to the train and Budd-built stainless steel observation cars appeared for the two trainsets made necessary for the revised schedule.

Old surplus *Mercury* equipment was refurbished at the Beech Grove Shops and then put in service between Detroit and Cincinnati as the *Cincinnati Mercury*. This despite the fact that its companion train had to be made up of standard equipment.

The *Cincinnati Mercury*, train 303 left Detroit at 11:30 every morning and arrived at Cincinnati Union Terminal at 6:00 p.m. Northbound, the train left

Cincinnati at 8:50 a.m. and arrived at Detroit's Michigan Central Station at 3:40 p.m. Stops included Wyandotte and Monroe, Michigan and Ohio cities of Toledo, Fostoria, Carey, Forest, Kenton, Bellefontaine, Urbana, Springfield, Dayton, Middletown, Cincinnati-Winton Place and downtown Cincinnati. The consist was the same as the original *Mercury* except for the lack of a straight parlor car.[15]

As dieselization overtook New York Central's passenger fleet, it was inevitable that steam power would disappear from the *Mercury* as well. Soon it was F-3 diesel locomotives that were backed down from the Linndale roundhouse to the westbound train. Then the stop at Linndale was eliminated and several minutes were cut from the schedule as a result.

The first *Mercury* casualty of the declining passenger business was the *Cincinnati Mercury*, the run from Cleveland to Cincinnati and return. This train had been established after B&O's streamlined *Cincinnatian* went into Cincinnati-Detroit service. The new B&O streamliner, however, proved to be too much competition for the paralleling New York Central route. The extra set of *Mercury* cars had been shifted to the Cleveland run, leaving Cleveland at 7:50 a.m., and arriving Cincinnati at 1:45 p.m. The train was powered by Niagara-type 4-8-4s. Then the low-slung experimental train *Xplorer* took over the schedule in an effort to stanch the flow of business oozing out to the highways. The *Cincinnati Mercury* gave up the ghoston June 23, 1956.

The *Chicago Mercury*, in the meantime, had been combined with the *Wolverine* and lost its name early in 1958.

The *Cleveland Mercury* lasted a bit longer, also being affected by a loss of business to the highway, principally the Ohio Turnpike. By the fall of 1956 the round end observation car had been removed and by the following spring the train was being equipped with standard streamlined coaches, diner, parlor car and lounge coach. A sleeping car from the *Cleveland Limited* as well as a companion New York-Toledo coach were spliced into the train upon arrival at Cleveland.

The *Mercury* was gone by July 11, 1959, just 23 years from its birth; a victim of the superhighways that promoted the automobile age to the detriment of the railroad. Gone were the classy *Mercury* locomotives and the posh *Mercury* streamlined cars, now all worn out. It had become just another train, still keeping a glorious name. And now it, too, was gone.

Only 79 persons rode that last *Mercury* from Cleveland. A passenger on that trip remembered the old *Mercury*: "You could work all day and then get on the *Mercury* (in Detroit) and relax," he recalled.

Conductor David A. Crossmier, assigned to the last run, who had been with the railroad for 43 years, spoke about happier times, such as the huge tips lucky gamblers would pass out after winning big in a *Mercury* compartment card game. He remembered the baseball players from the Cleveland Indians and the Detroit Tigers, movie and TV star Jack Webb, a strip teaser who gave him her colorfully illustrated "business" card and a Swedish ambassador who was delighted with the train.

A dining car employee wistfully remembered when it was necessary to have 23 men on duty to handle the food service aboard the train.

Also remembered was the time, at the height of the *Mercury's* popularity, when one had to reserve a seat two weeks in advance in order to get on the waiting list.[16]

The *Mercury*, winged messenger of the gods, made its mark on mid-America. Yesterday's delight as the "Train of Tomorrow" lives on in the fond memories of a diminishing corps of devotees—and in the written word and historical illustrations. The "Train of Tomorrow" was truly a train to be remembered!

Acknowledgements

I would like to extend my great thanks for their invaluable help in making this book more interesting to C. R. Bachmam, Ray S. Curl, Mrs. Zora Gumz, Emery Gulash, J. David Ingles, Bob Lorenz, George Snyder, Prof. Harry Stegmaier, Jay Williams, Lansing Vail and Bill Edson of the New York Central System Historical Society, and the Western Reserve Historical Society of Cleveland.

NOTES

1. Henry Dreyfuss, *Designing For People*, (New York, 1955), pp. 111-113.
2. *Plain Dealer*, Cleveland, Ohio, July 11, 1936.
3. *Ibid.*
4. *Cleveland News*, July 13, 1936.
5. *Railway Age*, July 11, 1936, p. 53.
6. *Ibid.*, p. 62.
7. *Railway Age*, November 7, 1936, p. 688.
8. *Plain Dealer*, July 16, 1936.
9. Henry Dreyfuss, *Designing For People*, p. 111.
10. *Ibid.*, p. 112.
11. *Railway Age*, *February* 13, 1937.
12. *Ibid.*, April 24, 1937.
13. *Plain Dealer*, August 1, 1938.
14. New York Central timetable for June 22, 1941.
15. Harry Stegmaier, Jr., "The Mercury," *Passenger Train Journal*, October, 1987.
16. *Plain Dealer*, "Mercury Crawls Into Terminal Tomb To Die," July 11, 1959.

Emery Gulash

The *Chicago Mercury*, Train 75, passes through Wayne, Mich., in April 1947. By this time the observation car had lost its skirting.

THE MERCURY LOCOMOTIVE

Richard J. Cook, Sr. Collection

NYC publicity photo shows *The Mercury* locomotive fresh from the West Albany erecting shop with its "bathtub" cowl. Note the absence of a number or marker lights, the train name under the cab window and large road name on the tender being the only marking.

NYC, NYCS Hist. Society

Henry Dreyfuss's plaster of Paris mock-up of the proposed *Mercury* Locomotive. The final product certainly matched the concept. Note the emphasized drivers, even on the model.

At the New York Central's West Albany Shops, the railroad took two Big Four K-5b locomotives and rebuilt them for service on the new Cleveland-Detroit Mercury streamliner. Here is another of the same type, No. 4914 (ex-6514), undergoing repairs at the Beech Grove Shops near Indianapolis.

J. H. Genders, Collection of Jay Williams

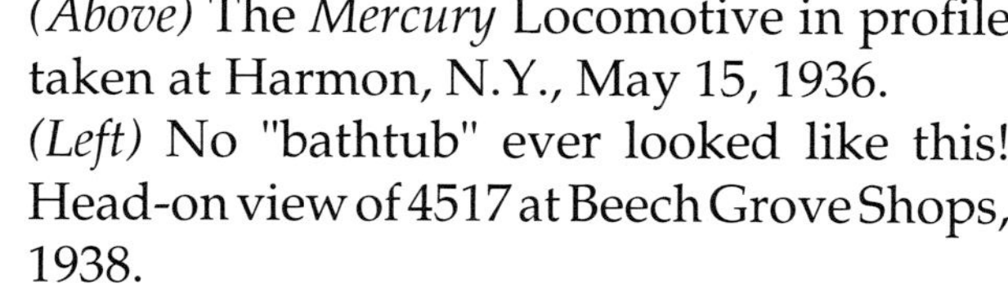

(Above) The *Mercury* Locomotive in profile taken at Harmon, N.Y., May 15, 1936.
(Left) No "bathtub" ever looked like this! Head-on view of 4517 at Beech Grove Shops, 1938.
(Right) Rear view of the *Mercury's* tender. Locomotive tenders on the NYC always carried individual numbers. The shape of the plating was tailored to blend in with the trailing train. Taken at Harmon, N. Y. May 15, 1936.
(Below) A drawing of the locomotive, showing lettering style and placement.

All Photos this page, NYC, NYC System Historical Society

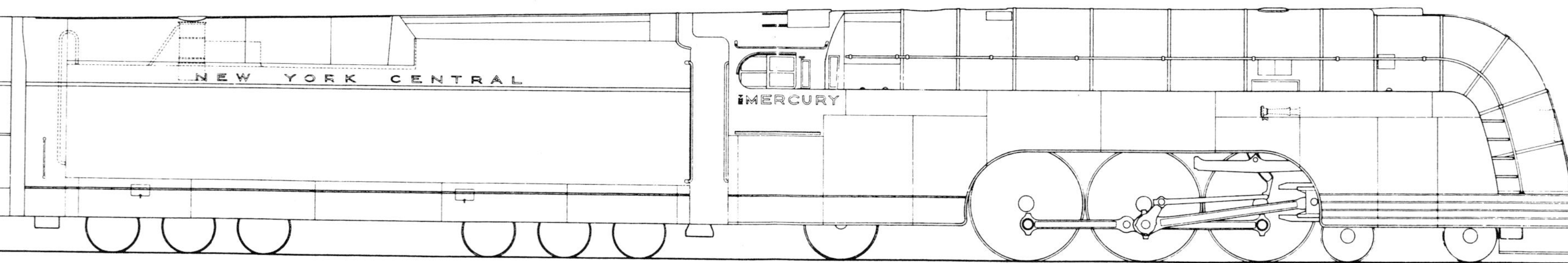

NYC, Richard J. Cook, Sr. Collection

At Beech Grove, September 1938. This was before the engine number was applied just below the cab window.

NYC, NYCS Hist. Society

The *Mercury's* locomotive made a impressive show even when at rest. Shown here at Harmon, N. Y. during the 1936 display tour.

Shorn of two plates of its cowl, the 4917 reveals some of its true nature in this 1936 photo.

NYC, NYCS Hist. Society

NYC, Richard J. Cook, Sr. Collection

New York Central power: the old and the new (1936), along the Hudson River in this publicity photo during the *Mercury's* pre-run New York publicity tour.

NYC, NYCS Hist. Society

In the time-honored pose, a coveralled engineer holds the throttle of the *Mercury* locomotive for the NYC publicity photographer in May 1936.

NYC, NYCS Hist. Society

No one who ever saw the *Mercury* at speed could ever forget those wonderful drivers, even more dramatic illuminated at night.

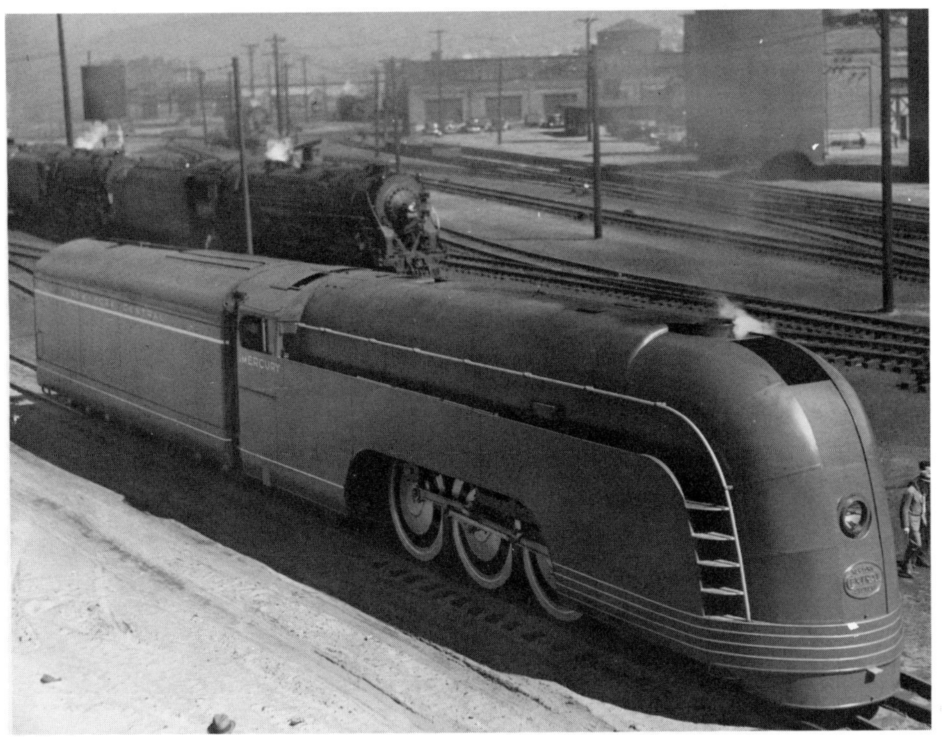

NYC, Richard J. Cook, Sr. Collection

Another publicity shot of the *Mercury* locomotive at Harmon, NY, gave an unusual overhead view which seems to emphasize the completeness of the streamlining. No hard corners or sharp angles here. Dreyfuss did what he could to lessen the air "drag" of the fast-moving machine.

THE MERCURY CARS

Ed Nowak photo; Richard J. Cook, Sr. Collection

The observation end of the *Mercury* at rest in Michigan Central Terminal, Detroit.

Henry Dreyfuss, faced with the cancellation of the *Mercury* project because of cost, suggested to NYC management that they refurbish older cars for the train rather than build or buy entirely new ones. This struck a responsive chord and the result was the refurbishment of ten-year old commuter cars for use in the *Mercury*. Of course, only the basic car body was used. The interiors were completely gutted and rebuilt to the new specifications and standards. Wide vestibules, skirting halfway down the truck frames, and Dreyfuss' s exterior paint treatment made the cars truly streamlined in appearance, though the riveted sides belied an earlier heritage.

NYC, Richard J. Cook, Sr. Collection

The original Mercury observation car, *Detroit*. This view shows the lower line of the observation windows, as well as the *Mercury* medallion, placed on each car, just to the right of the steps.

MERCURY PASSENGER EQUIPMENT

Car No.	Configuration	Orig. Blt.	Lot	Date Rebuilt	Orig. Car No.	Notes
1001	Baggage/52-seat Coach	1927	*OBC2093	1936	90	1
1002	60-seat Coach	1927	OBC2038	1936	2401	
1003	18-seat Coach/ Kitchen	1927	OBC2038	1936	2403	
1004	62-seat Diner	1927	OBC2038	1936	2405	
1005	56-seat Coach	1927	OBC2038	1936	2407	
1006	56-seat Coach	1927	OBC2038	1936	2415	
1007	Baggage/52-seat Coach	1927	OBC2093	1939	91	1
1008	60-seat Coach	1927	OBC2038	1939	3700	
1009	56-seat Coach	1927	OBC2038	1939	3703	
1010	56-seat Coach	1927	OBC2038	1939	3706	
1011	56-seat Coach	1927	OBC2038	1939	3708	
1012	56-seat Coach	1927	OBC2038	1939	3709	
1013	22-seat Coach/ Kitchen	1927	OBC2038	1939	3713	
1014	62-seat Diner	1927	OBC2038	1939	3714	
1015 *Toledo*	Buffet/Lounge	1927	OBC2038	1936	2424	2
1016 *Michigan*	Buffet/Lounge	1927	OBC2038	1939	3720	2
1017 *Cleveland*	Parlor	1927	OBC2038	1936	2427	2
1018 *Greenfield Village*	Parlor/Observation	1927	OBC2038	1939	3721	2
1019 *Detroit*	Parlor/Observation	1927	OBC2038	1936	2429	2
1020 *Chicago*	Parlor/Observation	1927	OBC2038	1939	3723	2

Notes: * "OBC" is Osgood Bradley Car. Co.

1. 1001 and 1007 made from suburban combines 90 and 91. All others were rebuilt suburban coaches.
2. Named Pullman-operated cars were not given numbers until 1952.

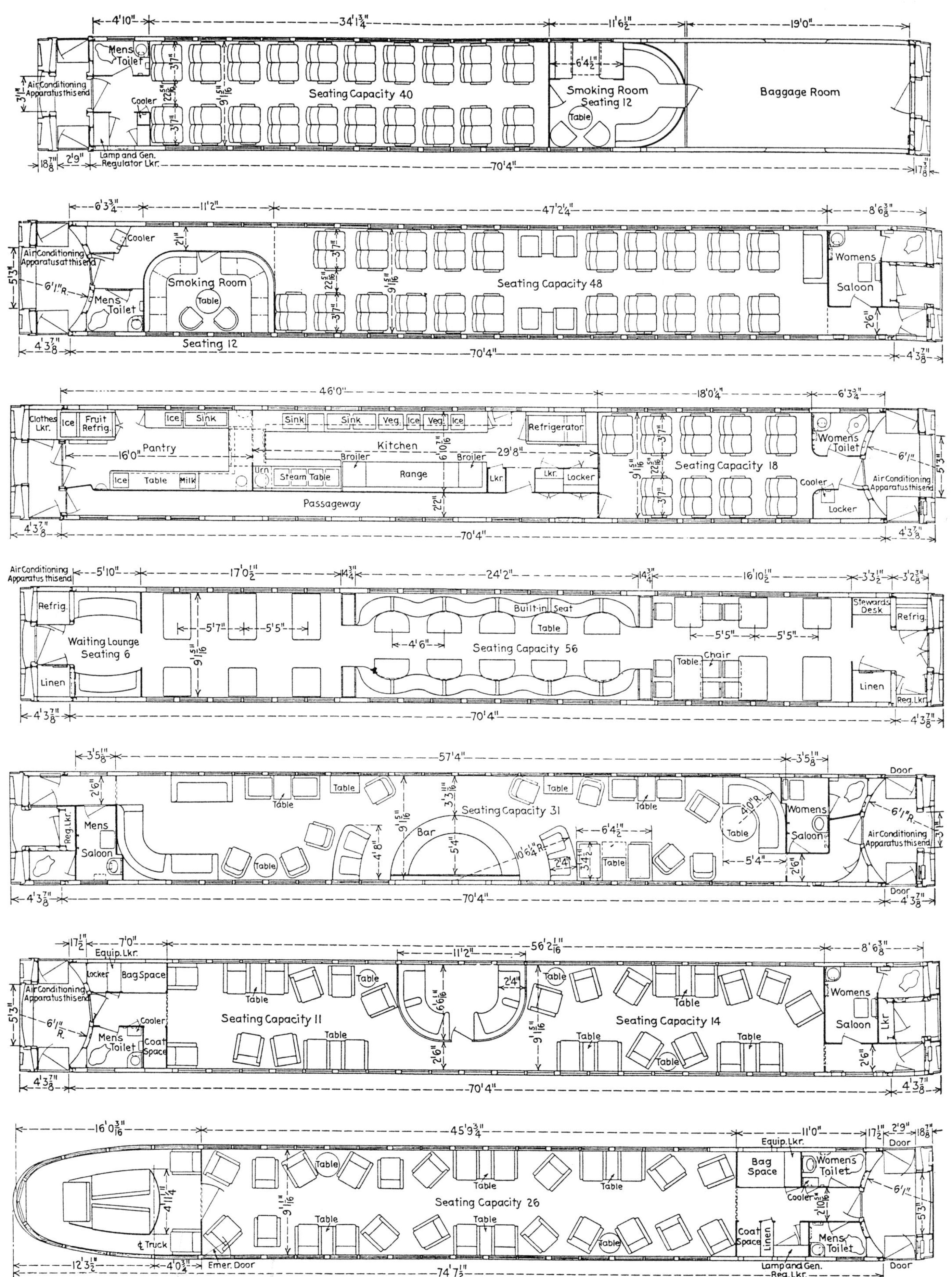

Floor plans for the original seven *Mercury* cars. (From *Railway Age*, July 11, 1936).

NYC, NYCS Hist. Society

NYC, NYCS Hist. Society

NYC Putnam Division commuter coaches looked like this before their conversion to *Mercury* equipment, a cost-saving move that allowed the train's creation. Above is car 3720 at Beech Grove Shops in 1939 just before its transformation into buffet/lounge car *Michigan* for the 1939 additions to the *Mercury* fleet. The interior at left is of car 3703 which became *Mercury* coach 1009.

Below, Mercury combination baggage/coach 1001 sits in Detroit's coach yard, easily distinguishable from other NYC equipment.

H. H. Harwood, Jr. Collection

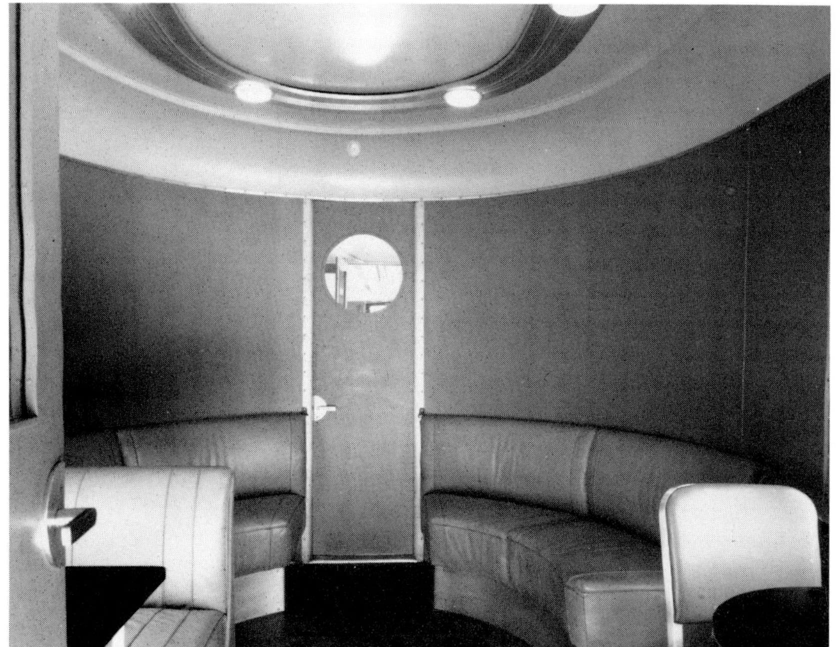

Looking toward the baggage compartment in the coach/baggage combination car. Note the circular lounge sofas and occasional chairs as well as a table provided for this smoking room.

NYC, NYCS Hist. Society

Official NYC Mechanical Diagram for the Combination Car.

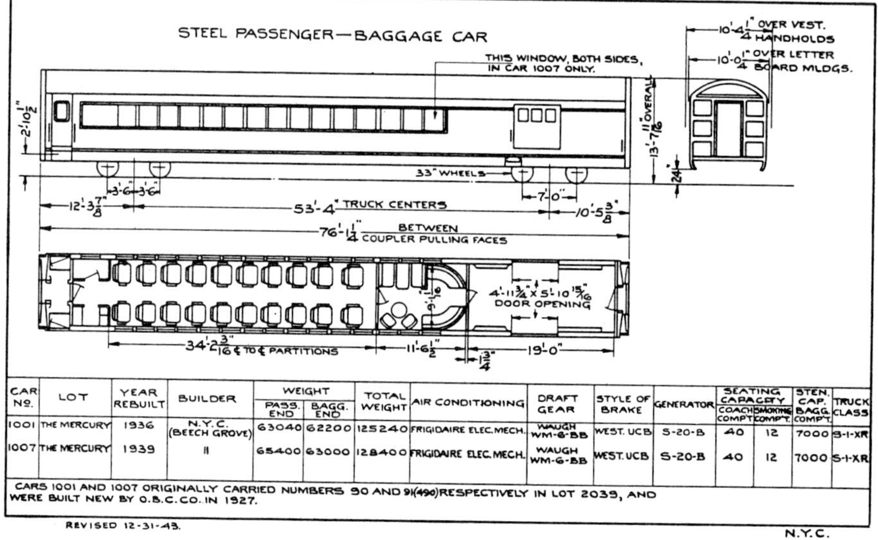

CAR Nº.	LOT	YEAR REBUILT	BUILDER	WEIGHT PASS. END	WEIGHT BAGG. END	TOTAL WEIGHT	AIR CONDITIONING	DRAFT GEAR	STYLE OF BRAKE	GENERATOR	SEATING CAPACITY COACH COMP'T	SEATING CAPACITY SMOKING COMP'T	STEN. CAP. BAGG. COMP'T	TRUCK CLASS
1001	THE MERCURY	1936	N.Y.C. (BEECH GROVE)	63040	62200	125240	FRIGIDAIRE ELEC. MECH.	WAUGH WM-6-BB	WEST. UCB	S-20-B	40	12	7000	S-1-XR
1007	THE MERCURY	1939	"	65400	63000	128400	FRIGIDAIRE ELEC. MECH.	WAUGH WM-6-BB	WEST. UCB	S-20-B	40	12	7000	S-1-XR

CARS 1001 AND 1007 ORIGINALLY CARRIED NUMBERS 90 AND 91(490) RESPECTIVELY IN LOT 2039, AND WERE BUILT NEW BY O.B.C.CO. IN 1927.

REVISED 12-31-43.

N.Y.C.

Bill Edson

The *Mercury* medallion and the wide vestibule/diaphragm curtain are aptly shown at Beech Grove in 1936.

NYC, NYCS Hist. Society

NYC, NYCS Hist. Society

New Mercury Coach 1005 at Beech Grove Shops December 19, 1936.

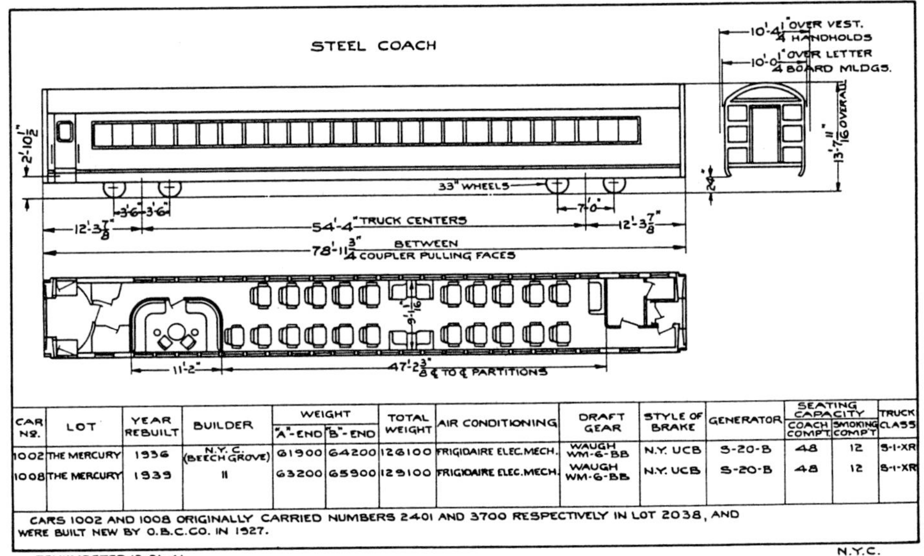

CAR No.	LOT	YEAR REBUILT	BUILDER	WEIGHT "A"-END	WEIGHT "B"-END	TOTAL WEIGHT	AIR CONDITIONING	DRAFT GEAR	STYLE OF BRAKE	GENERATOR	SEATING CAPACITY COACH COMPT.	SEATING CAPACITY SMOKING COMPT.	TRUCK CLASS
1002	THE MERCURY	1936	N.Y.C. (BEECH GROVE)	61900	64200	126100	FRIGIDAIRE ELEC. MECH.	WAUGH WM-6-BB	N.Y. UCB	S-20-B	48	12	S-1-XR
1008	THE MERCURY	1939	"	63200	65900	129100	FRIGIDAIRE ELEC. MECH.	WAUGH WM-6-BB	N.Y. UCB	S-20-B	48	12	S-1-XR

CARS 1002 AND 1008 ORIGINALLY CARRIED NUMBERS 2401 AND 3700 RESPECTIVELY IN LOT 2038, AND WERE BUILT NEW BY O.B.C.CO. IN 1927.

RENUMBERED 12-31-41.

N.Y.C.

Official NYC mechanical diagram for the *Mercury* coaches.

Bill Edson

Interior of coach, new at Beech Grove Dec. 19, 1936, shows table, lamp, and easy chairs that were located at mid-car, helping to break up the long aisle.

NYC, NYCS Hist. Society

NYC, NYCS Hist. Society

A coach with the famous Cleveland skyline photo-mural on the smoking room bulkhead.

1937 Car Builders Cyclopedia

Behind the photo-mural wall was this well appointed smoking room equipped with curved couch, free-standing chairs and table, as well as the obligatory heavy smoking stand of the era.

The famous circular *Mercury* vestibule. *(Above)* Passenger's view as he/she passed from one car to another. *(Right)* Exterior door (door to car interior at left) (design rendering). *(Below, left)* Designer's rendering of floor and ceiling plans. *(Below, right)* Door into the car interior from the vestibule (design rendering).

All illustrations this page courtesy NYC System Historical Society.

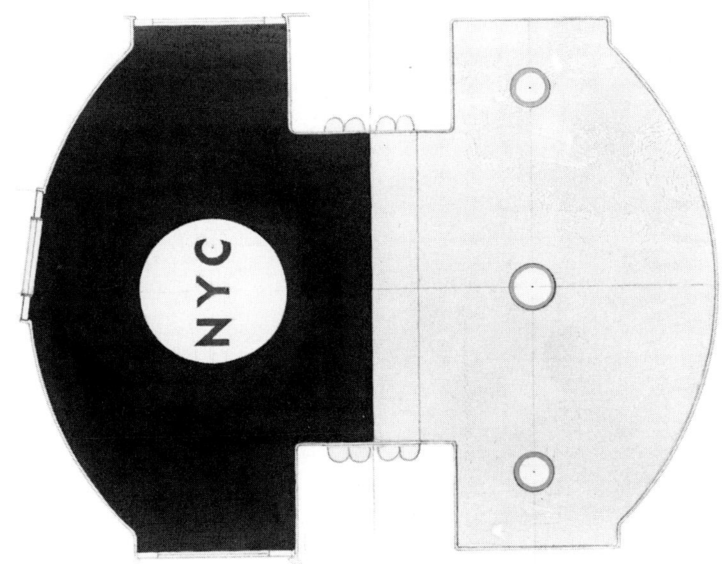

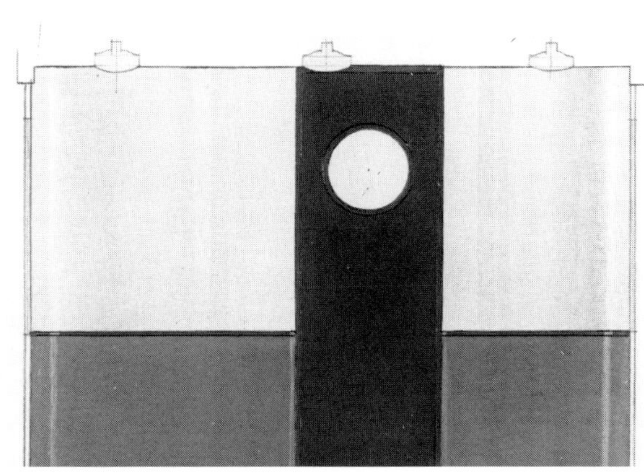

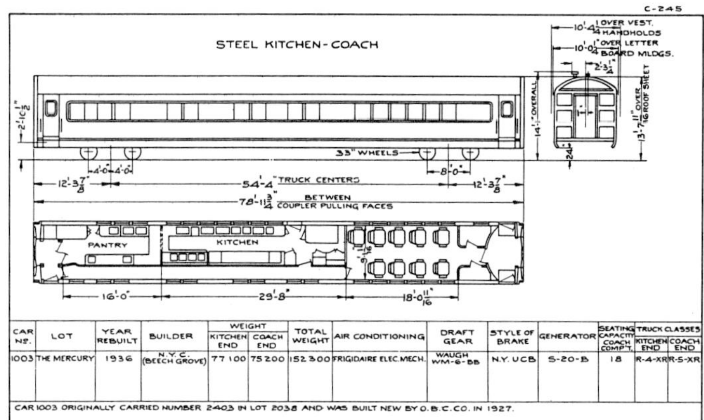

CAR Nº.	LOT	YEAR REBUILT	BUILDER	WEIGHT KITCHEN END	WEIGHT COACH END	TOTAL WEIGHT	AIR CONDITIONING	DRAFT GEAR	STYLE OF BRAKE	GENERATOR	SEATING CAPACITY COACH COMP'T.	TRUCK CLASSES KITCHEN END	TRUCK CLASSES COACH END
1003	THE MERCURY	1936	N.Y.C. (BEECH GROVE)	77 100	75 200	152 300	FRIGIDAIRE ELEC. MECH.	WAUGH WM-6-BB	N.Y. UCB	S-20-B	18	R-4-XR	R-5-XR

CAR 1003 ORIGINALLY CARRIED NUMBER 2403 IN LOT 2038 AND WAS BUILT NEW BY O.B.C. CO. IN 1927.

Diagrams (left and below) of the Mercury Kitchen/Dorm car and full Diner.

Both, Bill Edson

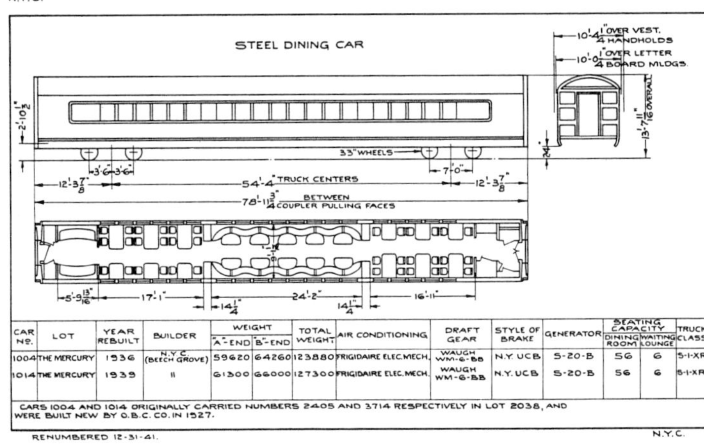

CAR Nº.	LOT	YEAR REBUILT	BUILDER	WEIGHT "A"-END	WEIGHT "B"-END	TOTAL WEIGHT	AIR CONDITIONING	DRAFT GEAR	STYLE OF BRAKE	GENERATOR	SEATING CAPACITY DINING ROOM	SEATING CAPACITY WAITING LOUNGE	TRUCK CLASS
1004	THE MERCURY	1936	N.Y.C. (BEECH GROVE)	59620	64260	123880	FRIGIDAIRE ELEC. MECH.	WAUGH WM-6-BB	N.Y. UCB	S-20-B	56	6	S-1-XR
1014	THE MERCURY	1939	"	61300	66000	127300	FRIGIDAIRE ELEC. MECH.	WAUGH WM-6-BB	N.Y. UCB	S-20-B	56	6	S-1-XR

CARS 1004 AND 1014 ORIGINALLY CARRIED NUMBERS 2405 AND 3714 RESPECTIVELY IN LOT 2038, AND WERE BUILT NEW BY O.B.C. CO. IN 1927.

Kitchen area of the Kitchen/Dormitory car, looking toward the pantry. The stainless steel fixtures are shining like silver.

NYC, Cleveland Press Collection, Cleveland State Univ.

NYC, NYCS Hist. Society

Diners enjoy a meal in the semi-circular, aisle-facing "Banquette" section of the *Mercury* diner, as aproned waiters attend.

For people waiting to be seated, this pleasant area was provided at one end of the diner, containing two plush couches and nicely decorated walls.

NYC, NYCS Hist. Society

NYC, George Snyder Collection

The semi-circular bar in the lounge car was the center of attention for many *Mercury* patrons.

NYC, NYCS Hist. Society

Parlor/Lounge attendant poses in his distinctive uniform in 1936. The parlor and lounge cars on the *Mercury* were operated by the Pullman Company.

The diagram shows *Mercury's* novel seating arrangement.

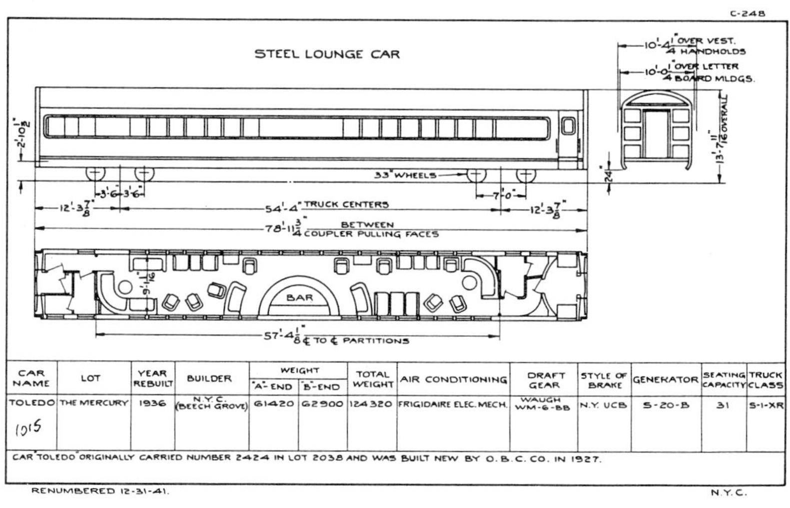

CAR NAME	LOT	YEAR REBUILT	BUILDER	WEIGHT "A" END	WEIGHT "B" END	TOTAL WEIGHT	AIR CONDITIONING	DRAFT GEAR	STYLE OF BRAKE	GENERATOR	SEATING CAPACITY	TRUCK CLASS
TOLEDO 1015	THE MERCURY	1936	N.Y.C. (BEECH GROVE)	61420	62900	124320	FRIGIDAIRE ELEC. MECH.	WAUGH WM-6-BB	N.Y. UCB	S-20-B	31	S-1-XR

CAR "TOLEDO" ORIGINALLY CARRIED NUMBER 2424 IN LOT 2038 AND WAS BUILT NEW BY O. B. C. CO. IN 1927.

RENUMBERED 12-31-41.

N.Y.C.

Bill Edson

NYC, NYCS Hist. Society

(Above) The famous cloud mural covers the curved bulkhead of the drawing room in the Mercury's Parlor car. *(Right)* Two 1936-era passengers sit in relaxed comfort, enjoying the then-innovative indirect lighting.

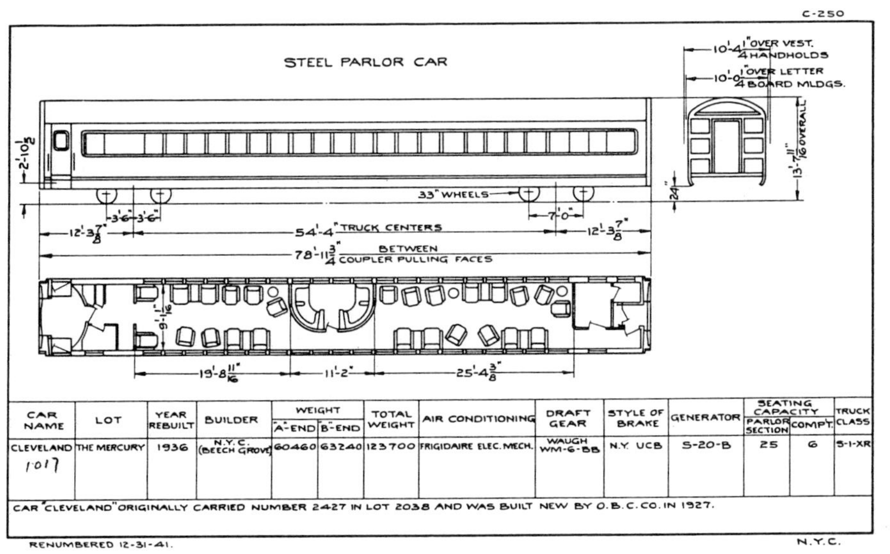

CAR NAME	LOT	YEAR REBUILT	BUILDER	WEIGHT		TOTAL WEIGHT	AIR CONDITIONING	DRAFT GEAR	STYLE OF BRAKE	GENERATOR	SEATING CAPACITY		TRUCK CLASS
				"A"-END	"B"-END						PARLOR SECTION	COMPT.	
CLEVELAND 1017	THE MERCURY	1936	N.Y.C. (BEECH GROVE)	60460	63240	123700	FRIGIDAIRE ELEC. MECH.	WAUGH WM-6-BB	N.Y. UCB	S-20-B	25	6	S-1-XR

CAR "CLEVELAND" ORIGINALLY CARRIED NUMBER 2427 IN LOT 2038 AND WAS BUILT NEW BY O.B.C.CO. IN 1927.

RENUMBERED 12-31-41. N.Y.C.

Bill Edson

The diagram above and the artist's rendering at right show the center-car compartment in the Parlor car that could accommodate up to six people in private comfort.

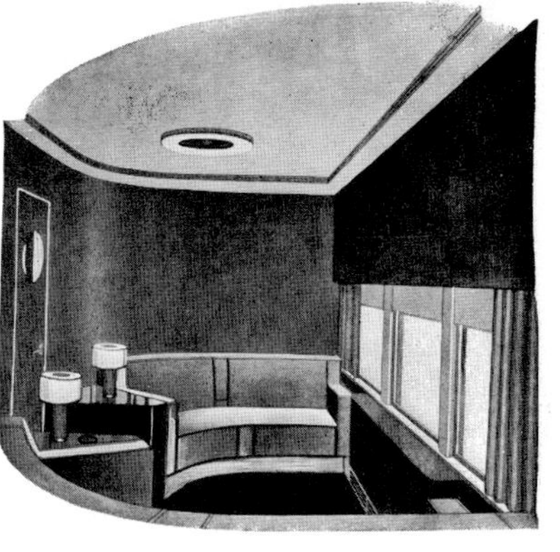

NYC, Coll. of Richard J. Cook, Sr.

Collection of Jay Williams

The observation car for the New York Central's *Pacemaker* (right), the road's all-coach train (to compete with the *Trail Blazer* of the Pennsylvania Railroad), was fashioned at the Beech Grove Shops from a regular coach. This rear end is typical of observation car ends and serves as a comparison to the lower, wider view windows of the *Mercury* observation cars (left). The wide-view *Mercury* observation served as a front-runner and model for later streamliners which utilized a much larger window space--much to the enjoyment of the scenery-viewing passengers.

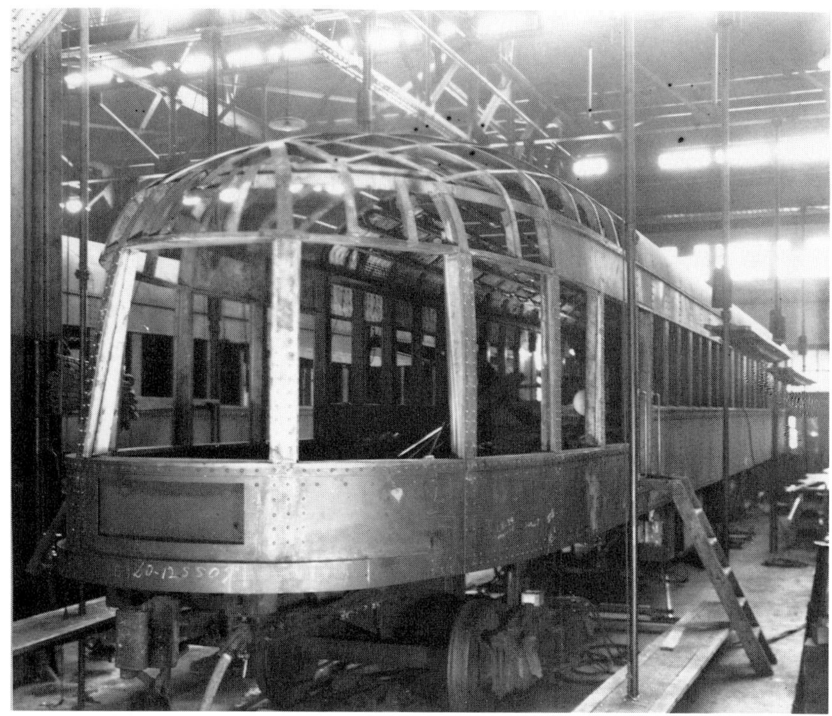

The *Mercury's* observation car in process of "streamlining" at Beech Grove Shops, near Indianapolis, Ind. The form of the old commuter car may be seen beyond the revamped portion.

NYC, NYCS Hist. Society

The observation car *Detroit* seated 30 comfortably. This view is looking forward from the rear end.

NYC, George Snyder Coll.

Looking the other way toward the observation end. Note the dramatic effect of the trough-mounted indirect lighting.

NYC, NYCS Hist. Society

THE MERCURY

" The Train of Tomorrow "

Streamlined — — Air-conditioned

All seats in coaches as well as parlor cars are reserved; individually assigned in advance and sold by number.

No. 75-750 —Lounge Car, Parlor Car, Parlor-Observation Car, Dining Car and Coaches Cleveland to Detroit.

No. 761-76 —Lounge Car, Parlor Car, Parlor-Observation Car, Dining Car and Coaches Detroit to Cleveland.

Timetable consist notes for the *Mercury*.

NYC, Richard J. Cook, Sr.

Sailor straw hats and a cigar typified the businessman summer traveler on the Detroit-bound train. This view shows the train at speed with Huron, Ohio fast receding in the distance from the vantage point of the observation car. The date is August 21, 1939.

NYC, NYCS Hist. Society

Blow up of speedometer mounted in the back of the settee in the observation section.

NYC, NYCS Hist. Society

(Above) The *Mercury* observation suffered damage when J-3a streamlined Hudson No. 5416 powering *The Commodore Vanderbilt* rear-ended it at Rocky Ridge, Ohio on July 30, 1938.

(Below) Dreyfuss's arrangement of seating in the observation car again employed some seats permanently attached to the walls and others that could swivel.

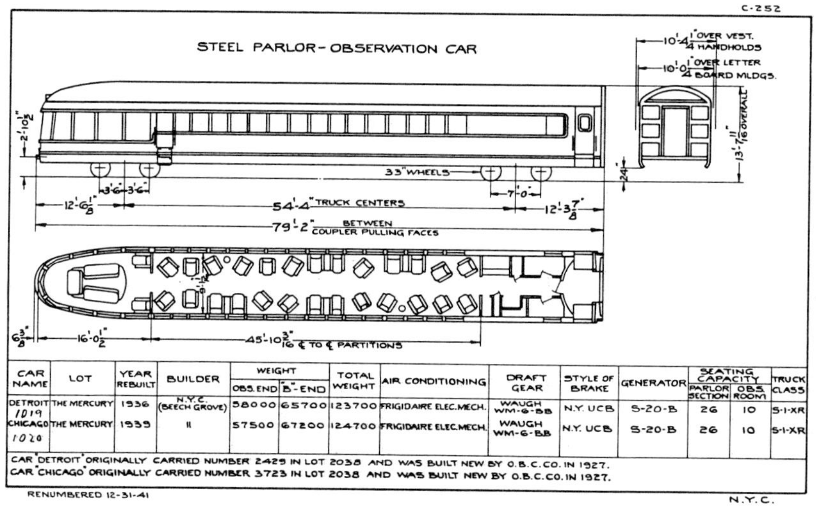

CAR NAME	LOT	YEAR REBUILT	BUILDER	WEIGHT		TOTAL WEIGHT	AIR CONDITIONING	DRAFT GEAR	STYLE OF BRAKE	GENERATOR	SEATING CAPACITY		TRUCK CLASS
				OBS. END	"B"-END						PARLOR SECTION	OBS. ROOM	
DETROIT 1019	THE MERCURY	1936	N.Y.C. (BEECH GROVE)	58000	65700	123700	FRIGIDAIRE ELEC. MECH.	WAUGH WM-6-BB	N.Y. UCB	S-20-B	26	10	S-1-XR
CHICAGO 1020	THE MERCURY	1939	"	57500	67200	124700	FRIGIDAIRE ELEC. MECH.	WAUGH WM-6-BB	N.Y. UCB	S-20-B	26	10	S-1-XR

CAR "DETROIT" ORIGINALLY CARRIED NUMBER 2429 IN LOT 2038 AND WAS BUILT NEW BY O.B.C.CO. IN 1927.
CAR "CHICAGO" ORIGINALLY CARRIED NUMBER 3723 IN LOT 2038 AND WAS BUILT NEW BY O.B.C.CO. IN 1927.

RENUMBERED 12-31-41

N.Y.C.

Bill Edson

THE MERCURY DEBUTS

NYC, NYCS Hist. Society

NYC, NYCS Hist. Society

On June 25, 1936 Miss Louise Landman, daughter of L. W. Landman, General Passenger Traffic Manager of the NYC used a bottle of champagne from Sandusky, Ohio, along the train's route to officially christen the *Mercury* at Indianapolis Union Station. (The train was built at Beech Grove, near Indianapolis, in the magnificent Big Four shops where today Amtrak maintains its nationwide passenger fleet.) An audience of straw-hatted gentlemen and conservatively dressed ladies looks on. That evening the train left for its display at New York on June 28 and 29.

C. B. Chaney, Collection of T. W. Dixon, Jr.

(Left) The 4915 (ex-6515) and the *Mercury* on exhibition in Grand Central Station, New York, in early 1936, before being placed in service.

(Below) The original seven-car train is shown in this much-circulated publicity photo of 1936.

NYC, Richard J. Cook, Sr. Collection

A study in contrasts: the *Mercury* engine and a standard Hudson-type passenger engine of the time. Taken at Harmon on the publicity tour.

NYC, Richard J. Cook Sr. Collection

Under the end of Cleveland Union Terminal.

Backing into the Terminal.

Crossing the Cuyahoga River bridge, just out of the Terminal.

Three views taken of the press run of the *Mercury* on July 13, 1936, by Robert C. Bachman, New York Central dispatcher.

NYC, NYCS Hist. Society

(Above) Professional photographer Robert Yarnell Ritchie tried an infra-red portrait of the *Mercury* easing through the switches at Michigan Central Terminal, Detroit, in the train's early days. This photo was never circulated widely.

The new *Mercury* rated a full-page ad in the September 25, 1938 New York Central/Michigan Central System public timetable, along with a plug for the diner.

Harry Stegmaier Collection

A MERCURY ALBUM

NYC, NYCS Hist. Society

A nine-car *Mercury* streaked westbound near Sandusky, Ohio, in 1938 but was stopped by the camera of Andrew Hriz. No. 4917 was doing the pulling honors.

Bob Lorenz

Here comes the *Mercury* at high speed, rushing past the platforms of the station at Port Clinton, Ohio in 1939, and bound for Cleveland.

Westbound out of Cleveland comes No. 75 on its morning flight to the Motor City, here at Brookpark Road on an April day in 1938, with No. 4917 at the business end.

NYC, Richard J, Cook, Sr. Collection

No. 75 was at full speed, passing the station at Port Clinton, Ohio, when this shot was taken in 1936.

Observation car of the westbound *Mercury* crosses Sandusky Bay at Bay Bridge, Ohio, Oct. 1, 1936.

NYC, NYCS Hist. Society

Richard J. Cook, Sr.

It was a rare thing when the *Mercury* was filled beyond capacity. But in the train's earlier years, especially during World War II when there just were no more *Mercury* cars, other equipment had to be found. That was the case on Memorial Day, 1942, when a second section was ordered up by the company to handle the Detroit-bound overflow. A combine baggage-coach, two conventional coaches, a streamlined coach and a parlor-observation car were the consist. One cannot help but wonder if passengers on this train were somewhat contented by the fact that one of the new *Twentieth Century* streamlined locomotives (No. 5445) strutted out in front of their abbreviated train. There can be no doubt that the 5445 kept her train right on the block of first 75.

At Detroit, a Cleveland-bound *Mercury* gets under way with Hudson 5351 and 15 cars, while B&O's *Ambassador* (right) waits its turn to begin its overnight run to Washington.

E. L. Thompson, Collection of H. H. Harwood, Jr.

The *Mercury* storms out of Detroit's Michigan Central Station, its imposing office-building headhouse obscured by exhaust, in April 1941.

Picking up speed, the *Mercury's* cars rattle over the switch points as the train threads its way out of the Detroit station yard.

A full load of passengers has already gathered in the observation car to watch the train's departure.

All three photos this page by H. H. Harwood, Sr., Collection of H. H. Harwood, Jr.

All aboard for Toledo! The *Mercury* got under way this May 10, 1947 with a standard Hudson-type (No. 5432) pulling 12 cars. The place is Linndale where the electric motor turned over the train to the Toledo Division engine and crew. The time is 8:05 a.m.

Richard J. Cook, Sr.

Richard J. Cook, Sr.

Eastbound *Mercury,* No. 76, swooped into Toledo on a slight downgrade on the Detroit-Toledo section of the route. A standard Hudson, No. 5355, was pulling a 12-car train on July 1, 1945 as the train passed the Spicer Manufacturing plant on Toledo's north side. Notice that the engineer had a greeting for the photographer. Behind the original *Mercury* combine may be seen five newer non-*Mercury* streamlined cars.

Richard J. Cook, Sr.

On May 28, 1953, a 10-car *Mercury* rushed up the grade past Clark Ave. (see roof of tower at left) on its way to Linndale and a change of power from electric to steam. Here motor No. 215 gets saluted by Guy Caruso and his section crew, almost lost in the shadows at the left. After the *Mercury* passed by the crew got back to work and the towerman was able to handle a few switching moves through his interlocking plant.

Richard J. Cook, Sr.

By 1950 (July 21 in this instance) the *Mercury's* heavier train was being handled by the Cleveland Union Terminal electric motors and Hudson-type steam locomotives west from Linndale. Here, just outside the Terminal structure, the *Mercury* is under way up the grade with 10 *Mercury* cars in its consist. It appears that already one passenger has taken advantage of the unsurpassed view afforded by the *Mercury's* observation lounge. He'll see a lot of fascinating railroading by the time he gets to Detroit!

One type of diesel assigned to the *Mercury* in the early diesel power period was steam heat-equipped GP-7, No. 5794. These Geeps were used for only a short time in such service. No. 75, here, is just leaving Linndale, Ohio, on its run to Detroit on a November day in 1953.

Bill Edson

F-3 No. 3502, a regular in the *Mercury* service is shown here about to leave Cleveland Union Terminal with No. 75, just as Nickel Plate's No. 6, *The Nickel Plate Limited,* arrives from Chicago.

Early in the diesel era the *Mercury* was assigned class DCA/DCB passenger-equipped F-3s in three sets: 3500/3600(AB),3501/3601(AB), 3502/3503(AA) on a 3-day cycle. A set would take No. 75 Cleveland-Detroit and return on No.76, then would handle other trains Cleveland-Chicago-Buffalo-Cleveland during the next two days, returning to No. 75 and 76 on the third day. These units were converted to freight service about 1958.

Al Staufer

The *Mercury* arrives at Michigan Central Station, Detroit, as shown in this 1937 rear-end photo.

Glenn Grabill, Collection of H. H. Harwood, Jr.

Howard Ameling Collection

The *Cleveland Mercury*, No. 76, is eastbound near Huron, Ohio, at about 8:00 p. m. on a July evening in 1954 with Erie Built Fairbanks-Morse No. 4505 for power and only one non-*Mercury* car in the consist.

Bob Lorenz Collection

At Detroit the engine crew gets ready to take the 4917 from the roundhouse to the Michigan Central Terminal where it will couple onto its Cleveland-bound train.

THE CHICAGO MERCURY

R. P. Longanacre, NYCS Hist. Society

The Chicago-Detroit *Mercury* at speed with a streamlined Hudson up front in October 1940.

The New

MERCURY

The most distinguished day train in America is now in service between

CHICAGO and DETROIT

via Michigan Central Route

SCHEDULE—*Chicago and Detroit*

Eastbound	
Lv. Chicago, Central Station *Michigan Ave. & Roosevelt Road*	9:00 A.M.(C.T.)
Lv. Chicago, 63rd St. Station	9:09 A.M.(C.T.)
Lv. Niles	11:34 A.M.(E.T.)
Lv. Kalamazoo	12:22 P.M.(E.T.)
Lv. Battle Creek	12:46 P.M.(E.T.)
Lv. Jackson	1:31 P.M.(E.T.)
Lv. Ann Arbor	2:08 P.M.(E.T.)
Ar. Detroit, Michigan Central Station	2:45 P.M.(E.T.)
Westbound	
Lv. Detroit, Michigan Central Station	1:00 P.M.(E.T.)
Lv. Ann Arbor	1:37 P.M.(E.T.)
Lv. Jackson	2:14 P.M.(E.T.)
Lv. Battle Creek	2:59 P.M.(E.T.)
Lv. Kalamazoo	3:25 P.M.(E.T.)
Lv. Niles	4:11 P.M.(E.T.)
Ar. Chicago, 63rd St. Station	4:36 P.M.(C.T.)
Ar. Chicago, Central Station *Michigan Ave. & Roosevelt Road*	4:45 P.M.(C.T.)

1939 *Chicago Mercury* ad and timetable.

H. H. Harwood Collection

Eastbound out of Central Station in Chicago, on a November day in 1939, comes the new Detroit-bound *Mercury*, pulled by twice-streamlined Hudson 5344, greeting the morning sunlight and digging in for a fast 10-minute trip down Illinois Central's multi-tracked main line; first stop 63rd Street, Woodlawn. Then west over Michigan Central rails through Gary and Michigan City and on into Michigan.

Train 75, the *Chicago Mercury* with J-1d class Hudson No. 5301 westbound between Detroit and Dearborn, Mich., May of 1941.

Ed Nowak, Collection of Richard J. Cook, Sr.

Elmer Treloar, Collection of Jay Williams

In 1948 the Detroit-Chicago *Mercury* -- at least on this day -- looked nothing like the *Mercury* train at all because its power was the Hudson-type locomotive especially designed for the *Empire State Express*. This is No. 75 passing through Dearborn, Mich., on July 25, 1948.

Jay Williams Collection

Another photo showing *Empire State Express* Hudson No. 5426 with "The Mercury" plaque on the pilot over the New York Central oval. Train No. 75 is at Niles, Mich., probably in 1948.

This view of the Detroit-Chicago *Mercury* is unusual in two ways. First, it is seen under the wires of the Illinois Central's suburban electrified system and, secondly, it is powered by Hudson No. 5344, the first streamlined Hudson that the Central ran, the "Commodore Vanderbilt," but now with a new streamlining job to blend in with the later J-3a 5400-series Hudsons. It was said that the 5344 was the only steam locomotive in the country to boast two different streamlinings. Photo taken December 1939.

NYC, NYCS Hist. Society

The Michigan Central's *Mercury*, No. 76, Detroit-bound, stopped at the Ann Arbor, Mich. station on a football Saturday, Nov. 24, 1945. After a heavy exchange of passengers, the engineer is watching for his signal from the rear end to highball into Detroit with Hudson-type No. 5355.

Richard J. Cook, Sr.

Westbound to Chicago, the *Mercury* slides through Dearborn, Mich., in August 1940.

Emery Gulash

The *Mercury* with original equipment, roaring west through Dearborn in August 1940. Streamlined Hudsons were assigned to the *Chicago Mercury* almost from the beginning.

Emery Gulash

The *Mercury* is headed by non-streamlined Hudson 5345 on October 1, 1946, as it crosses Sandusky Bay at Sandusky, Ohio.

Ed Nowak, NYC

For a time, the Hudson 5429, originally the streamlined *Empire State Express* locomotive, was assigned to the *Mercury* and had a plaque lettered "The Mercury" placed over the NYC logo on the solid cast pilot for its run between Detroit and Chicago, shown here at Eloise, Mich. in 1947.

Emery Gulash

Eastbound, east of Ann Arbor, Mich., the Detroit-bound *Chicago Mercury*, with a non-streamlined Hudson, was caught by the camera of Emery Gulash.

Emery Gulash

With *Empire State Express* Hudson No. 5429 up front, The *Mercury*, No. 75, roars through Wayne, Mich. in 1947.

Emery Gulash

Richard J. Cook, Sr.

The *Chicago Mercury*, No. 75, thunders through Porter, Ind., at 4:00 p. m. on June 28, 1942. Streamlined Hudson No. 5445 is running with a light stack on the downgrade.

An E-7 and an E-8 have an 11-car *Mercury* in tow passing a track gang at Dowagiac, Mich., June 23, 1954. The original *Mercury* cars have all been displaced by stainless steel coaches, and there is even a heavyweight express car in the consist. The years of the *Mercury* service were numbered on this bright spring day.

NYC, NYCS Hist. Society

THE CINCINNATI MERCURY

Simon E. Herring; Collection of Jay Williams

The short-lived Cleveland-Cincinnati *Mercury* usually drew Central's largest passenger power, a 4-8-4 Niagara-type. Here at Bellefontaine, Ohio, the Cincinnati-bound train, with some of the original *Mercury* cars, is headed by S-1a class No. 6005 in 1955.

Bill Edson

(Left) A Fairbanks-Morse unit, No. 4506, was assigned to the *Cincinnati Mercury* on August 27, 1953. Here it has the 12-car southbound train passing beneath the Big Four coal dock at Galion, Ohio.

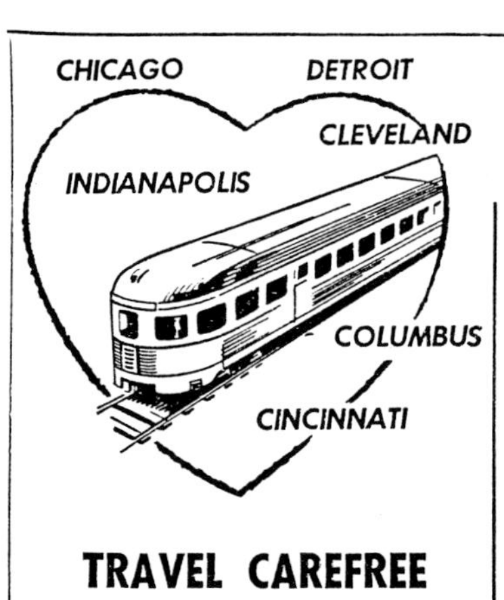

TRAVEL CAREFREE BY DAY THROUGH THE "HEART of the MID-WEST"

CHICAGO MERCURY
Parlor observation—streamlined diner — coach tavern lounge—reserved seat coaches. Mornings east and west, CHICAGO—DETROIT.

TWILIGHT LIMITED
Late afternoon twin of the morning **Mercury.**

CLEVELAND MERCURY
Parlor observation car, reserved-seat coaches, tavern lounge, diner. CLEVELAND to DETROIT morning; return afternoons.

CINCINNATI MERCURY
Parlor observation car, coaches with center smoking lounges, diner. Mornings, CLEVELAND to CINCINNATI; return afternoons.

JAMES WHITCOMB RILEY
All-reserved-seat coach streamliner. Coach observation car. Famous dining service. Mornings, CINCINNATI-CHICAGO; return afternoons.

(Right) This ad appeared in the April 24, 1955 New York Central System timetable, explaining all the *Mercury* services as well as the *James Whitcomb Riley*.

H. H. Harwood, Jr.

(Above) No. 421, the *Cincinnati Mercury*, was stopped at a signal at Cold Spring, Ohio, on an August day in 1953, not long before diesel power would take over from this non-streamlined Hudson. Notice that this edition of the *Mercury*, which left Cleveland at 7:50 each morning, carried a Railway Post Office car.

(Below) The *Mercury*'s observation car is shown in Cincinnati Union Terminal at the end of its run from Cleveland, in August 1953.

H. H. Harwood, Jr.

THE JAMES WHITCOMB RILEY

Richard J. Cook, Sr. Collection

(Above) The *James Whitcomb Riley* at Brent, Indiana, with probably the 4917, with the *Mercury* cowl but Big Four Standard marker lights breaking up streamlining of the nose. One of the innovations of the *Mercury* locomotive design was a smoke-deflector that lifted exhaust high above the speeding train and away from the cars. *(Below)* A Riley advertising blotter with timetable.

Bill Edson Collection

The 4917 as the *Riley* engine at Indianapolis Union Station in 1940.

Lamar M. Kelly Photo; T. W. Dixon, Jr. Collection

Jay Williams Collection

Ex-*Mercury* locomotives 4915 and 4917 are seen here at Indianapolis at the west end of the station.

The *Mercury* equipment, now called the *James Whitcomb Riley*, was displayed at such on-line cities between Cincinnati and Chicago as Indianapolis, Lafayette, and Kankakee.

Bill Edson

MERCURY DINING SERVICE

The Mercury was a totally integrated design: locomotive, cars, interiors, and even the china used in the diner were Dreyfuss-designed. The diner itself was probably one of the most unconventional designs ever attempted with its "banquette" section in the center where patrons were arranged with backs to the car walls before semi-circular tables. The plate glass green-houses that separated the center section from the two more conventionally-arranged dining areas and the reception area, where passengers could be seated on comfortable sofas while waiting to be seated in the diner, all combined to make breakfast or dinner on the *Mercury* an unforgettable experience. In this symphony of style the china, too, played its part, and has today become well known among collectors.

Richard J. Cook, Sr.

Dreyfuss-designed *Mercury* china for the New York Central may still be found today. Here are a few representative pieces. From left: bouillon cup; celery dish, bread plate and coffee mug. This has proved to be one of the most striking and popular designs of dining car china.

NYC, NYCS Hist. Society

One of the standard 4-person tables in the *Mercury* Diner is set with Dreyfuss-styled china and silver flatware and holloware.

Much comment was made on the varied seating arrangements in the *Mercury* dining car, which included a section of conventional two and four-person tables at each end and the "banquette" center section with unique semi-circular tables which faced the aisle. Dinner on the *Mercury* was an experience to be savored and long remembered.

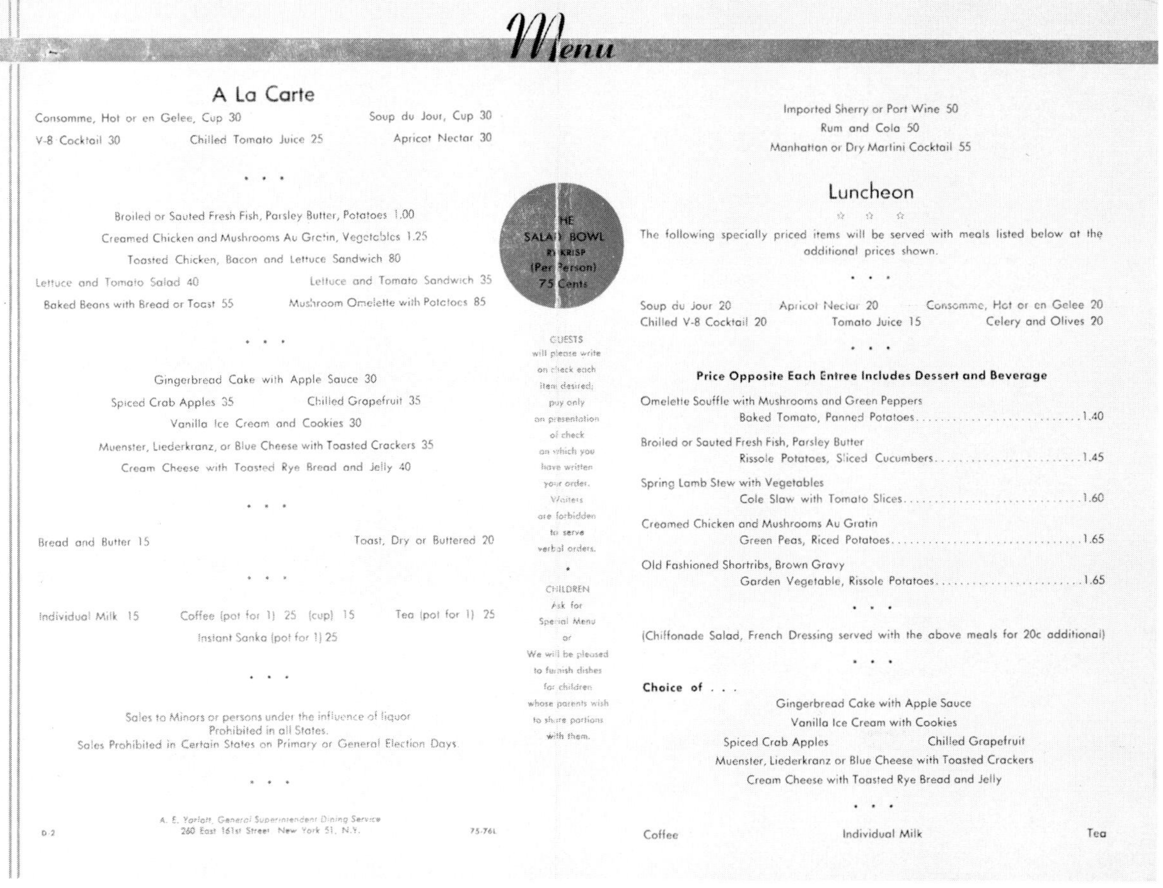

Menu

A La Carte

Consomme, Hot or en Gelee, Cup 30 — Soup du Jour, Cup 30
V-8 Cocktail 30 — Chilled Tomato Juice 25 — Apricot Nectar 30

. . .

Broiled or Sauted Fresh Fish, Parsley Butter, Potatoes 1.00
Creamed Chicken and Mushrooms Au Gratin, Vegetables 1.25
Toasted Chicken, Bacon and Lettuce Sandwich 80
Lettuce and Tomato Salad 40 — Lettuce and Tomato Sandwich 35
Baked Beans with Bread or Toast 55 — Mushroom Omelette with Potatoes 85

. . .

Gingerbread Cake with Apple Sauce 30
Spiced Crab Apples 35 — Chilled Grapefruit 35
Vanilla Ice Cream and Cookies 30
Muenster, Liederkranz, or Blue Cheese with Toasted Crackers 35
Cream Cheese with Toasted Rye Bread and Jelly 40

. . .

Bread and Butter 15 — Toast, Dry or Buttered 20

. . .

Individual Milk 15 — Coffee (pot for 1) 25 (cup) 15 — Tea (pot for 1) 25
Instant Sanka (pot for 1) 25

. . .

Sales to Minors or persons under the influence of liquor
Prohibited in all States.
Sales Prohibited in Certain States on Primary or General Election Days.

. . .

D-2 — A. E. Yarlott, General Superintendent Dining Service, 260 East 161st Street New York 51, N.Y. — 75-76L

HE SALA BOWL R KRISP (Per Person) 75 Cents

GUESTS will please write on check each item desired; pay only on presentation of check on which you have written your order. Waiters are forbidden to serve verbal orders.

CHILDREN Ask for Special Menu or We will be pleased to furnish dishes for children whose parents wish to share portions with them.

Imported Sherry or Port Wine 50
Rum and Cola 50
Manhattan or Dry Martini Cocktail 55

Luncheon

☆ ☆ ☆

The following specially priced items will be served with meals listed below at the additional prices shown.

. . .

Soup du Jour 20 — Apricot Nectar 20 — Consomme, Hot or en Gelee 20
Chilled V-8 Cocktail 20 — Tomato Juice 15 — Celery and Olives 20

. . .

Price Opposite Each Entree Includes Dessert and Beverage

Omelette Souffle with Mushrooms and Green Peppers
Baked Tomato, Panned Potatoes 1.40

Broiled or Sauted Fresh Fish, Parsley Butter
Rissole Potatoes, Sliced Cucumbers 1.45

Spring Lamb Stew with Vegetables
Cole Slaw with Tomato Slices 1.60

Creamed Chicken and Mushrooms Au Gratin
Green Peas, Riced Potatoes 1.65

Old Fashioned Shortribs, Brown Gravy
Garden Vegetable, Rissole Potatoes 1.65

. . .

(Chiffonade Salad, French Dressing served with the above meals for 20c additional)

. . .

Choice of . . .

Gingerbread Cake with Apple Sauce
Vanilla Ice Cream with Cookies
Spiced Crab Apples — Chilled Grapefruit
Muenster, Liederkranz or Blue Cheese with Toasted Crackers
Cream Cheese with Toasted Rye Bread and Jelly

. . .

Coffee — Individual Milk — Tea

Harry Stegmaier Collection

The stylish *Mercury* Menu folder offered selections as tempting now as they were then.

CLEVELAND UNION TERMINAL THE MERCURY'S HOME

Richard J. Cook, Sr.

Cleveland Union Terminal was 'home' for the original *Mercury* trains as they left there early in the morning and returned in the evening after a hard day's work carrying passengers to and from Detroit.

The 708-foot-high Terminal Tower, the most visible part of the Union Terminal complex, has been one of the trademarks of Cleveland since it was opened in 1930. One of the last great union stations built in America (only Cincinnati and Los Angeles were later), it embodied all the optimism and confidence of the 1920s of a growing and expanding America. It has survived the Great Depression, World War II, and, most surprising, the end of railroad passenger service.

The complex comprised a steam railroad terminal and interurban terminal at and below street level, and a series of huge office structures above ground. The tower itself hosted the Van Sweringen brothers, who built the structure as the nerve center of their massive railroad empire of the 1920s. It long served as head office for the Van's own Nickel Plate and Chesapeake & Ohio Railways, the latter having vacated only in 1987. At the time it was built, the terminal complex was the largest group of office buildings under one management in the world.

Today the *Mercury* and all its counterparts are gone, but the rapid transit lines remain and can be expected to grow, the office space is among the most desirable in the city, and the tower is now becoming the central star in an area of grand revival for the city.

It was in this opulent, perhaps overbuilt, and certainly visionary terminal, that the *Mercury* was born and died, 1936-1959.

Cleveland Press Photo; George Snyder Collection

The gate was opened in Cleveland's Union Terminal and crowds of eager passengers descended to train 75 below. Clevelanders loved to ride the *Mercury*.

Aerial view of Terminal Tower complex as it looked in the 1940s. (From a post-card view)